THE GUMMI BEA

GUM OF MY BE
FRIENDS . . .

Also available:
The Gummi Bears 2: Gummi in a Gilded Cage
The Gummi Bears 3: The Secret of the Juice
The Gummi Bears 4: Light Makes Right

THE GUMMI BEARS 1

GUM OF MY BEST FRIENDS . . .

TARGET

A TARGET BOOK
published by
the Paperback Division of
W.H. Allen & Co. Plc

A Target Book
Published in 1986
by the Paperback Division of.
W.H. Allen & Co. Plc
44 Hill Street, London W1X 8LB

Typeset by Phoenix Photosetting, Chatham
Printed and bound in Great Britain by
Scotprint Ltd, Musselburgh, Scotland

ISBN 0 426 20265 1

This is Cavin. He always believed in Gummi Bears although everyone else thought they were just a legend.

When he finally met them he was overjoyed. At last his dreams had come true!

There was Grammi, Gruffi, Zummi, Tummi, Sunni and Cubbi, and they all became Cavin's best friends.

The great secret of the Gummi Bears is Gummiberry Juice.

It can make Gummi Bears bounce very high . . .

. . . and make humans very, very strong.

This is the evil Duke Igthorn.

He planned to attack the castle of good King Gregor

with a mighty catapult.

‘We must help,’ said Cavin. ‘King Gregor is a good man!’

So Cavin and the Gummi Bears set off to rescue King Gregor.

Gruffi was soon captured by a terrible Ogre.

‘Don’t worry,’ said Cavin. ‘I’ll save you!’ And he drank a bottle of Gummiberry Juice.

The Ogre didn’t stand a chance!

'Look!' said Cavin. 'Igthorn is attacking the castle!'

Crash! A boulder smashed into the castle wall.

But Cavin used his super strength . . .

. . . and managed to send the catapult crashing down to the ground!

King Gregor was saved and Cavin was a hero!

Late that night the Gummi Bears wrote in their secret book: *Today we helped a young boy save his kingdom.*